Blue Shoes

ANGELA BULL

Illustrated by Jacqui Thomas

Oxford University Press

OXFORD
UNIVERSITY PRESS

Great Clarendon Street, Oxford OX2 6DP

Oxford University Press is a department of the University of Oxford.
It furthers the University's objective of excellence in research, scholarship,
and education by publishing worldwide in

Oxford New York

Auckland Bangkok Buenos Aires Cape Town Chennai
Dar es Salaam Delhi Hong Kong Istanbul Karachi Kolkata
Kuala Lumpur Madrid Melbourne Mexico City Mumbai Nairobi
São Paulo Shanghai Taipei Tokyo Toronto

Oxford is a registered trade mark of Oxford University Press
in the UK and in certain other countries

ISBN 0 19 916909 8   School edition
ISBN 0 19 918514 X   Bookshop edition

Printed in Great Britain by Ebenezer Baylis

Illustrations by Jacqui Thomas c/o Linda Rogers Associates

Photograph of Angela Bull by courtesy of the Craven Herald

For Emily

Chapter 1

Lucy and Mum sat in the shoe shop.
Around them lay piles of new shoes.

'Which do you like best?' asked
Mum.

Lucy sighed. She didn't like *any* of
them. They all looked the same. You
could see hundreds just like them
walking up and down the High Street
any day. Lucy didn't want to be the
same as everyone else.

'I hate all these boring shoes,' she said.

'Don't be difficult please, Lucy,' Mum said. 'You must have some new shoes, and that's that.'

Lucy looked round the shop again, and suddenly she saw them!

She knew at once that they were the shoes she wanted. They were blue and shiny, with patterns of tiny flowers on them, and they were quite different from any other shoes in the shop.

Special! That's what they were. Really special!

They stood on a glass shelf, waiting for Lucy.

'Could I try those blue ones?' she asked Mum eagerly.

The blue shoes gleamed on her feet. They were a bit tight, but that didn't matter. They looked perfect.

'They're rather posh,' said Mum. 'I meant to buy you something for every day.' She felt Lucy's toes through the shoes. 'Are you sure they fit?'

'Yes! Oh, yes!' said Lucy. 'Can I wear them for the Christmas Fair?'

'All right,' said Mum.

Chapter 2

It was the school's Christmas Fair that afternoon. The whole family, Holly and Lucy, Peter and Robin, Mum and Dad, crammed into the car and drove to the school.

They parked in the playground where Peter often played football at lunchtime.

'Goal!' Peter shouted, pretending to kick a ball.

Lucy looked down at his scruffy old trainers with their red laces, and then at her own beautiful blue shoes. She felt like a princess as she walked into the school hall.

'Hey, Lucy, I love your shoes!' called her friend, Anna.

Lucy smiled and smiled. She walked slowly round the hall, taking care no one trod on her feet. It was good to feel so special – even if the shoes *were* a bit tight.

On a table sat a big toy dog. It was made of glossy brown fur, and it had a red bow round its neck. All the family stopped to look at it.

'Isn't it fantastic?' said Lucy.

'It's the sort of dog Aunty Sue makes,' said Holly.

Aunty Sue had a craft shop, and Holly loved the wonderful things she made for it.

'You have to guess the dog's name,' explained a teacher, who was sitting behind the table. 'If you choose the right one, you win him. You pick a name from this list.'

'I'll try Lassie,' said Holly.

'I bet it'll be White Fang,' said Peter.

'Bobbie,' chose Robin, because it sounded a bit like his name.

'You're all wrong,' Lucy told them. 'It's Scooby-Doo to rhyme with my blue shoe.'

Holly, Peter and Robin laughed. How could Lucy's new shoes have anything to do with the toy dog's name?

But what a surprise! When the head teacher called out the prizes, Lucy had won. The dog really was called Scooby-Doo. Everyone clapped as Lucy went forward to collect it.

'It's my new shoes,' she said. 'I think they must be lucky.'

All the same, she was glad to take them off when she got home. They'd rubbed a blister on her big toe. Lucy decided not to tell Mum. Perhaps the new shoes would fit better the next time.

'I'll only wear them for special things,' she told Holly, as she put them away in the cupboard.

It was surprising how good her boring old trainers felt, when she slipped them on instead.

Chapter 3

Very soon, another special thing
happened. All the family went to the
pantomime.

'You can wear your new shoes,'
Holly told Lucy, when they were
getting ready.

'Yes, I'm going to,' said Lucy.

She took them out of the cupboard,
and put them on. They felt *nearly* all
right.

Lucy enjoyed the pantomime so much, she forgot about her shoes. Halfway through, a magician came on stage.

'Now then,' he began, 'I want someone to come up here and help me.'

All the children jumped about, and waved their arms. They hoped he would choose them.

The magician looked down. He
pointed to Lucy.

'I'll have you,' he said.

Lucy squeezed along the row, and
ran up on to the stage.

'Why is Lucy so lucky?' grumbled
Peter.

'It must be those blue shoes,' said
Robin.

The magician made Lucy stand in
the middle of the stage. Then he
waved his wand. He began pulling
things out of her pockets, out of her
sleeves, and even out of her ears.

There were coloured hankies and
streamers, fluttering feathers and
strings of glittering beads. Soon, they
were lying in heaps round her feet.

The magician glanced down and
waved his wand again. Out of the blue
shoes came two, huge, blue fans.

'How did you do that?' gasped Lucy.

'It's magic,' said the magician. 'But those shoes of yours are something special. I guess they'll bring you lots of luck.'

Everyone clapped as Lucy went back to her place.

'Shoes can't bring luck,' said Holly
sensibly, as they were going home.

'Lucy's have,' Peter pointed out. 'She
won Scooby-Doo, *and* she got chosen
to help the magician.'

'She was wearing her blue shoes
both times,' squeaked Robin.

'So they must be lucky,' said Peter.

Lucy didn't say anything. She felt half excited by the idea, but half scared too. She liked her shoes, but she wasn't sure she wanted them to be magical. It made them feel rather dangerous. Most of all, she wished they didn't hurt so much.

As soon as she got home, she took them off. Then she sneaked a bit of plaster from the bathroom cupboard, and wrapped it round her blistered toe.

It was funny, but the moment she pulled on her sloppy old trainers felt like the best moment of the day.

Even Mum seemed to think the blue shoes were lucky. Lucy heard her on the phone, chatting to Aunty Sue.

'First the dog, and then going on stage,' she was saying. 'I wonder what will happen to Lucy next?'

Chapter 4

What happened to Lucy next was that
Aunty Sue asked to see her new shoes.

'We'll call at the craft shop
tomorrow,' said Mum.

So next morning, Lucy put on the
blue shoes again. With the plaster
round her toe, they didn't feel at all
bad.

I think they're starting to fit me, Lucy
decided.

She felt very happy as she set off with Mum and Holly, Peter and Robin.

Aunty Sue thought the shoes were beautiful.

'I'd love a pair like that,' she said. 'I'd fill them with blue and silver dried flowers, and hang them on the wall.'

'You can't have these,' said Lucy. 'Sorry. They're mine.'

At that moment a lady came into the shop. She needed a basket for her dog which had just had puppies.

'Something roomy,' she told Aunty Sue, 'with plenty of cushions.'

Aunty Sue lifted down several baskets. Lucy watched her, wondering if the puppies looked like Scooby-Doo.

'This is my niece, Lucy,' said Aunty Sue to the lady. 'Lucy, this is Mrs Robinson.'

Mrs Robinson smiled at Lucy.

'Do you like dogs?' she asked.

'Yes, but I've only got a toy one,' said Lucy.

'I want to find homes for my puppies,' Mrs Robinson explained. 'Would you like to have one?'

'Me? A real puppy! Oh, Mum, can I?' cried Lucy.

'Yes! Go on, Mum! Let's have a puppy,' shouted Holly and Peter and Robin.

'Well – ' began Mum. Then she smiled. 'All right. Dad and I have been thinking it would be fun to have a dog.'

'Thank you,' said Lucy, to Mrs Robinson and Mum. 'It can be a real, live Scooby-Doo.'

Robin's eyes opened wide as saucers.

'I know why we're getting a puppy!' he said. 'Lucy's wearing her blue shoes.'

'Great! Let's go to lots of shops,' said Peter.

But Lucy was beginning to feel scared. Maybe the shoes really *were* lucky. The toy dog, the real one, and the chance to go on stage were all fantastic things. Only it would have been nicer and safer if they'd happened in an ordinary way, and not because of a pair of shoes.

The shoes were starting to hurt again too. Lucy wished she could take them off. But Mrs Robinson said they could go and look at the puppies, and of course, Holly and Peter and Robin couldn't wait.

So, wriggling her toes to try and find a less tight spot, Lucy followed the others to Mrs Robinson's car.

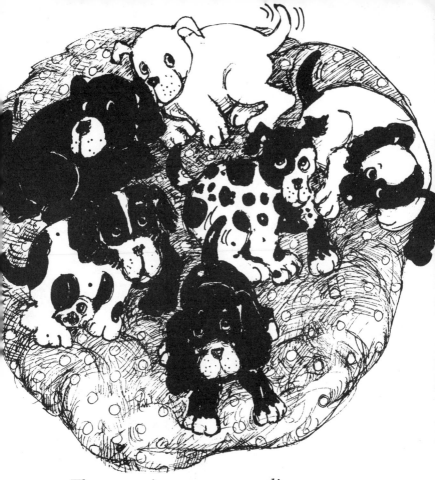

The puppies were sprawling on a
beanbag, in a tangle of silky brown
fur.

'Aren't they like Lucy's Scooby-Doo!'
cried Holly.

'I can't even see them properly,'
complained Robin.

'They always huddle together in a lump,' said Mrs Robinson.

'How can we choose?' wondered Peter.

At that moment one puppy squirmed out of the heap. It rolled across the beanbag, and pushed its nose into Lucy's hand.

'Look at that!' said Mrs Robinson. 'The puppy's chosen you. You can have him as soon as he's old enough to leave his mother. I think I know who his favourite person will be.'

'They'll *all* be favourites,' said Mum quickly.

But Peter and Robin were staring at Lucy's feet.

'Those lucky shoes *again*,' they muttered.

Chapter 5

Back home, Lucy put on her old
trainers, but she had to wear the blue
shoes for Gran's Christmas party.

Usually, she loved dressing up. This
time she felt miserable. It wasn't just
that the shoes hurt her toes. She
didn't like the way they were taking
charge of her life. She made up her
mind to forget them when she got
to Gran's.

At Gran's Christmas party there were always games. The first was a kind of treasure hunt.

Hidden round the sitting room were odd things, like a stick of spaghetti, a wooden spoon, and a rubber band. The first person to see where they all were, won the game.

Lucy began to look hard. If she thought about the game, she wouldn't be able to worry about her shoes.

She found the spaghetti stuck to a picture frame, the wooden spoon in a plant pot, the rubber band round the door knob, and all the other things.

'Finished!' she shouted.

'Oh, no! Not already,' groaned Holly
and Peter and Robin.

'I bet you haven't seen the
spaghetti,' said Peter.

'I have,' said Lucy.

'I've only found half the things,'
sighed Holly.

'I don't think we should have let
Lucy play,' said Robin.

'Why?' asked Aunty Sue.

'She's wearing her blue shoes, and they always make her lucky,' Robin explained.

'So it's not fair,' added Peter.

'That's rubbish!' said Gran and she handed Lucy her prize. It was a chocolate mouse.

But instead of feeling pleased, Lucy blinked back a tear.

Peter and Robin were wrong. The blue shoes had nothing to do with it. She'd won the prize with her sharp eyes, not her poor, sore feet – only they'd never believe that now.

Suddenly she hated her special blue shoes.

'Next,' said Gran, 'we'll play the remembering game.'

She showed them a tray with tiny objects on it. Everyone looked at it for two minutes. Then Gran covered the tray, and everyone made a list of the things they could remember.

I'm not going to win, thought Lucy. So she didn't try to remember. She just wrote a list of silly, impossible things.

Aunty Sue was sitting next to Lucy.
She glanced over Lucy's shoulder in
surprise.

'What a funny list!' she whispered.

'I don't want to win,' Lucy
whispered back.

'Why not?'

'It's my shoes,' Lucy whispered.
'When I wear them, lucky things keep
happening to me. That sounds nice,
but it isn't.'

Lucy went on, 'I won the treasure hunt properly, *and* Scooby-Doo at the Christmas Fair, but everyone thinks it was only because I was wearing my blue shoes. I feel as if they're taking over.'

'They're pretty,' murmured Aunty Sue.

'Yes,' agreed Lucy, 'but – they're terribly tight.'

'Hey!' called Dad. 'That's enough whispering.'

Then Gran uncovered the tray for them to check their lists. Lucy was glad to come last.

'Shoes wearing out?' teased Peter.

But Aunty Sue beckoned Lucy into a corner.

'Can we do a swap?' she said. 'If you let me have your blue shoes to sell in the craft shop, I'll get you a nice new pair.'

'Oh!' gasped Lucy. 'A new pair of shoes! That would be the luckiest thing of all.'

'Right!' said Aunty Sue. 'It's a deal.'

Next morning, Lucy and Aunty Sue sat in the shoe shop. Around them lay piles of new shoes.

'I made two lovely decorations when I filled your blue shoes with dried flowers,' said Aunty Sue. 'Now, which of these shoes do you like best?'

Lucy eyed the shoes. It was funny. They all looked special, in their own way. No wonder everyone walked up and down the High Street in them.

'Choose whichever you want,' said Aunty Sue.

Lucy's hand swooped down on a pair of green shoes with red edging.

'These!' she said happily.

About the author

When I was a little girl,
clothes and shoes were very
dull. I wore brown, buttoned
shoes in winter and brown
sandals in summer. I never
had a blue or red pair until
I was grown up. So, when I
had a daughter, I always
wanted her to have pretty shoes.

Once, we were asked to a special family party
and I let her choose some high-heeled blue
sandals. They looked beautiful, but they were
horribly tight. She never wore them again!

I live in the country in Yorkshire and I've
written lots of children's books.